Original title:
Yondered Wicks Among the Faerie Pest

Author: Liisi Lendorav
ISBN HARDBACK: 978-1-80563-163-7
ISBN PAPERBACK: 978-1-80564-684-6

## Secrets Illuminated in the Forest's Embrace

In shadows deep where whispers dwell,  A hidden path
allured my spell.  The ancient trees, they creak and sigh,
Beneath their limbs, old secrets lie.

With every step, the silence grew,  A shimmer danced on
mossy dew.  With cautious heart and bated breath,  I felt
the pull of silence, death.

A breeze would scatter tales of yore,  While spirits
lingered by the door.  Their murmurs twirled in twilight
time,  Each note a hidden, haunting rhyme.

The forest breathed with ancient lore,  As night
descended, thoughts would soar.  I marveled at this mystic
space,  Where nature held its warm embrace.

So here I stand, where dreams take flight,  Embraced by
shadows, kissed by night.  The world beyond shall fade
away,  In this secret glade where fairies play.

# Glowing Wonders Beneath the Veil of Stars

The night unfurl'd its velvet cloak,  Each twinkling light,
a whispered joke.  Beneath the stars, the secrets weave,  A
tapestry, fate's hand does cleave.

The moon's soft glow, a watchful eye,  As dreams arise
and spirits fly.  In midnight's throne, the wishes gleam,
Each twinkling star, a whispered dream.

I wander 'neath the cosmic dance,  Enchanted by each
fleeting chance.  The iron gates of dawn still close,  As
night's embrace, a fairytale grows.

With every sigh, a wish takes flight,  Beneath the sheen of
silver light.  Each glow, each spark, a promise made,  In
starlit skies, my heart won't fade.

Here in the night, I lose all care,  The universe sings, a
symphony rare.  A wondrous world beneath the stars,
Where dreams are born, no matter how far.

## The Fireflies' Serenade in the Mystic Dell

In twilight's glow, they start to dance,  The fireflies sway,
a flick'ring trance.  A melody of whispers low,  In fragrant
air where soft winds blow.

Through verdant leaves, their lights entwine,  As nature
hums a tune divine.  Each gleam a note, a flicker bright,
A serenade to greet the night.

The hush about, a sacred space,  Where magic lingers,
finds its place.  They twinkle where the shadows loom,  In
every blink, a heart's soft bloom.

I sit absorbed in this warm glow,  With every pulse, my
spirit's flow.  Each flicker paints a fleeting smile,  A bond
of souls, though just a while.

In the mystic dell where dreams align,  The fireflies spin
tales so fine.  Their song remains, a gentle plea,  In
nature's heart, forever free.

### Flickers of Magic in a Glade Adorned

In emerald hues, where wildflowers sway,  A magic
whispers, softly at play.  The glade adorned with dew's
embrace,  Each petal holds a dream's sweet trace.

A rustle, a giggle, the fairies appear,  With twinkling eyes
and joy sincere.  They dance on beams of sunlight's grace,
In this hidden, enchanted place.

Winds carry secrets, soft and light,  The glimmering
sprites fill day and night.  With laughter bright, they leap
and glide,  In every shadow, they gently bide.

The glade pulses with life so rare,  With every thought,
our spirits share.  Their fluttering wings bring tales of old,
In every spark, a magic bold.

As evening falls and stars descend,  The glade's allure
shall not soon end.  For here in peace, dreams intertwine,
In flickers of magic, the world aligns.

# Flare of the Faerie Lantern's Grasp

In a glen where shadows play,
The lanterns light the faerie way.
Glittering sparks in midnight's air,
Whisper secrets, weave a snare.

Their glow enchants the gentle night,
Telling tales of ancient flight.
Each flicker dances, soft and bright,
Guiding lost souls to delight.

Beneath the stars, they hum a tune,
Filling hearts with gentle swoon.
In every flick, a story weaves,
Crafted by the silent leaves.

The faerie folk, with laughter clear,
Draw you close, dispel your fear.
The lanterns pulse with magic's hand,
Creating wonder, ever grand.

In their grasp, the world stands still,
Embracing dreams, urging will.
With every glow, a promise shines,
In faerie realms, where magic twines.

# Glowing Threads in a Tapestry of Dreams

In realms where hopes and visions blend,
A tapestry stretches, never to end.
Threads of silver, gold, and blue,
Whisper secrets known to few.

Each stitch a promise, softly sewn,
Binding hearts to love once known.
Glimmers weave through night and day,
Painting dreams along the way.

A gentle touch, a thread pulled tight,
Guiding souls through darkest night.
Moments captured, colors swirled,
Creating magic, breathing worlds.

In this land of woven light,
Hearts entwine, taking flight.
With every glow, a story borne,
New beginnings, hope reborn.

So wander forth, brave heart aflame,
Seek the threads that call your name.
For in this place where dreams conspire,
Weave your wishes, build your fire.

## Ethereal Gleams on Silvered Wings

Beneath the moon's caress so sweet,
Creatures dance on silken feet.
Ethereal wings in twilight gleam,
Carrying whispers of a dream.

Fairy folk in circles spin,
Echoes of laughter rise within.
Glistening trails on starlit air,
Heartfelt moments, beyond compare.

Each flutter bright, a story told,
A testament of love so bold.
With every beat, the night expands,
Softly cradled in magic's hands.

As shadows wane, the night ignites,
Silvered wings in endless flights.
They carry hopes upon the breeze,
Awakening dreams among the trees.

So close your eyes and listen near,
To whispers only you can hear.
For in the night, with wings unfurled,
Ethereal wonders fill the world.

## Mirthful Glows Between the Boughs

Between the trees, a laughter springs,
A chorus formed of tiny wings.
Mirthful glows in playful dance,
Inviting all to take a chance.

Fireflies wink with spirited glee,
Lighting paths where hearts roam free.
With every flicker, joy takes flight,
Merging day with the gentle night.

In secret nooks, an echo rings,
The warmth of friendship softly clings.
Beneath the boughs, all sorrows cease,
As laughter weaves a thread of peace.

The night unfolds, a tapestry,
Of glowing faces, wild and free.
In every corner, life abounds,
Where merriment and magic surrounds.

So gather close, let spirits soar,
Embrace the night with hearts that roar.
For in this space between the trees,
Mirthful glows dance on the breeze.

# Gleaming Threads of Enchantment

In the heart of the forest, whispers entwine,
Golden threads of magic, glimmering divine.
With every soft rustle, a secret revealed,
Worlds hidden from vision, at last unsealed.

Underneath the moonlight, shadows take flight,
Dancing with fairies, igniting the night.
Each glow a reminder, of stories long told,
Of heroes and wonders, more precious than gold.

Lost in the tapestry, colors so bright,
Weaving through memories, a wondrous sight.
In every new dawn, enchantment will stay,
Gleaming threads of tales, guiding our way.

Beneath ancient oaks, the magic will gleam,
Life flows like water, a shimmering dream.
Collect the soft echoes, let them run free,
Gleaming threads of enchantment, forever will be.

In the warmth of our hearts, the magic ignites,
A tapestry golden, spun from our nights.
With laughter and whispers, we share our delight,
Gleaming threads of enchantment, our fate intertwined.

## Flickers of Magic on the Still Waters

On the lake's quiet surface, the moon's sweet glow,
Flickers of magic dance, gentle and slow.
Each ripple a whisper of stories once lost,
In the stillness of twilight, enchantment embossed.

Reflections of dreams drift softly and free,
Woven with starlight, a shimmering sea.
Nature's soft murmur, a spellbinding call,
Flickers of magic, weaving over all.

Eyes closed in wonder, the heart starts to sing,
Moments of silence, the joy they will bring.
With every new flicker, old tales come alive,
In the hush of the night, where memories thrive.

Candles of starlight flicker and sway,
In the cradle of nighttime, they softly play.
With each gentle ripple, the world welcomes you,
Flickers of magic on waters so blue.

So let your soul wander, where dreams intertwine,
Find solace in shadows, let the magic shine.
In the still of the night, let your spirit be free,
Flickers of magic, the heart's reverie.

## Chasing Glimmers through Twilight Mist

As dusk falls upon the horizon's embrace,
Chasing glimmers of light, through time and space.
The mist wraps around like a silken shawl,
Mysterious whispers, inviting us all.

In the twilight's soft glow, shadows will twirl,
Awakening visions, let fantasies whirl.
Through meadows of emerald, secrets unfold,
Chasing glimmers of magic, fierce and bold.

Each footstep a story, each breath a new thread,
In the dance of the night, where imaginations spread.
Through the veil of the mist, adventures ignite,
Chasing glimmers together, hearts filled with light.

With laughter like chimes, we wander and roam,
In the tapestry of twilight, we find our true home.
Each glimmer a beacon, lighting the path,
Chasing dreams in the mist, escaping the past.

So let us keep chasing, these glimmers we find,
Moments of wonder, forever intertwined.
Through twilight and mist, we'll bravely explore,
Chasing glimmers of magic, forevermore.

## The Glow of Forgotten Realms

In the corners of time, where shadows reside,
The glow of forgotten realms, ever our guide.
Whispers of tales lost, echo in dreams,
A mosaic of magic, alive at the seams.

Beneath ancient arches, where secrets hide,
The pulse of the past, a current inside.
With each gentle breeze, stories take flight,
The glow of forgotten realms beckons the night.

In the heart of the forest, where old oaks stand tall,
Shadows weave stories that summon us all.
Each flicker of starlight ignites yearning hearts,
The glow of forgotten realms, where wonder imparts.

Dreamers and seekers, with courage to roam,
Find solace in wonders, crafting a home.
In laughter and starlight, we gather as one,
The glow of forgotten realms, where journeys begun.

So cherish the moments, let magic renew,
In the glow of forgotten realms, we'll ever pursue.
Through whispers of twilight, our spirits shall rise,
Where the glow of forgotten realms opens our eyes.

# Enigmatic Flickers of the Unknown

In shadows deep, where secrets stir,
A whisper waltzes, soft and blurred.
Curiosity, a gold-tipped key,
Unlocking realms where none can see.

Flickers dance in twilight's glow,
Guiding hearts where few dare go.
They shimmer bright, these fleeting lights,
Eager souls in shadowed nights.

Within the mist, old tales unfold,
Of treasure lost and prophecies told.
An echo here, a laugh from there,
The unknown calls; it lures with flair.

Each spark a tale of yore recast,
With threads of fate, they weave so fast.
What lies ahead in veils so thin?
Embrace the whispers, let dreams begin.

Venture forth where the wild winds blow,
And capture hope in every glow.
For in the dark, a truth you'll find,
Enigmatic flickers, wondrous, unconfined.

## Twilight Fireflies in the Meadow's Heart

As twilight falls, the meadow wakes,
With fireflies dancing, gentle flakes.
They trace the paths of whispered lore,
In every flicker, dreams explore.

Golden glow on emerald blades,
A symphony that never fades.
They twirl in pirouettes of light,
Guiding wanderers through the night.

Each glimmer weaves a tender thread,
Of tales unsung and words unsaid.
Memory's touch, so soft and sweet,
Lures the heart in rhythmic beat.

In this embrace of day's retreat,
The nightingale sings, a voice discreet.
With every spark, the shadows fade,
As fireflies dance in twilight's shade.

So linger here, where magic stirs,
Amongst the glow, the quiet purrs.
In the meadow's heart, love takes flight,
With twilight fireflies, pure delight.

## Beacons of Light in Eldritch Woods

In eldritch woods where old trees sigh,
Beacons of light weave through the sky.
They beckon softly, drawing near,
A promise wrapped in whispered cheer.

Among the ferns, where shadows play,
A lantern flickers, guiding stray.
With every gleam, worlds intertwine,
Secrets lost in whispers divine.

As dusk descends with velvet grace,
Illuminated dreams embrace.
A spark ignites in hearts so bold,
Among these woods, tales are retold.

Here time stands still, a breathless pause,
In the embrace of ancient laws.
With glowing orbs, the brave shall tread,
To find the paths where few have bled.

So wander on, let courage reign,
Through mist and dew, through joy and pain.
In eldritch woods, together we'll stride,
With beacons of light, our hearts as guide.

# Shimmering Starlings in the Midst of Wonder

Amidst the veil of starlit skies,
Shimmering starlings take to rise.
A flurry of wings, a dance so free,
In the tapestry of night's decree.

With every flutter, a tale is spun,
Of journeys vast, of battles won.
Chasing dreams on the breath of night,
Echoing wishes, pure and bright.

In twilight's hush, they weave a song,
Where all the heartbeats truly belong.
With whispers soft and laughter clear,
They gather hopes, they draw us near.

A chorus calls, an urge to fly,
Through realms of wonder, up to the sky.
In shimmering throngs, we join their flight,
Captured by beauty, lost in the light.

So let your spirit join the throng,
In the dance of starlings, find where you belong.
In midst of wonder, let hearts entwine,
With shimmering grace, love shall align.

## Secrets of the Wicks beneath the Trees

In twilight's embrace, shadows arise,
Beneath old boughs, where the mystery lies.
Whispers of wicks, a flickering glow,
Guard ancient secrets that only they know.

Through tangled roots and mossy stones,
Echoes of laughter, familiar tones.
A dance of the fireflies, wild and bright,
Leading the lost through the veil of night.

The trees stand watch, in silence they greet,
The tales of the forest, the heartbeat discreet.
With each passing breeze, a soft refrain,
Of love and heartache, of joy and pain.

Hidden within, the past intertwines,
With shadows that stretch and twist like vines.
Memory lingers, sweet on the air,
In the glow of the wicks, a promise laid bare.

Beware the allure of the soft, warm light,
For it may ensnare you on this fateful night.
Yet seek the truth in the heart of the woods,
Where secrets and wonders nest in the hoods.

# Echoes of Light Beneath the Canopy

Beneath a quilt of green, softly sighs,
The forest holds echoes, where magic lies.
Gentle beams slip through, tracing their grace,
The dance of the leaves in a sweet embrace.

Every rustle reveals a tale hidden deep,
In shadows that cradle the secrets we keep.
A symphony sings through the dusk-warmed air,
Of moments forgotten, of dreams laid bare.

The wild thickets breathe with a life of their own,
As sunlight weaves patterns, like seeds overgrown.
Luminous whispers in corners of night,
A testament forged in the warm, tender light.

With each step we take on this earthen floor,
The magic of ages grows rich at its core.
Reality blurs, as we wander and roam,
In the echoing light, we find ourselves home.

So linger a while, let the magic unfold,
In the heart of the woods, where stories are told.
As lanterns ignite in the hush of the trees,
Echoes of light drift on welcoming breeze.

## The Dance of Flickering Faery Spirits

In glimmers of dusk, where shadows entwine,
The faery spirits begin to align.
They twirl and they leap, with laughter so bright,
A ballet of wonders beneath the soft night.

With wings made of starlight, they sparkle and glow,
Drawing us closer to the magic they sow.
Their whispers create a soft lullaby,
That beckons the dreamers and lures the shy.

The moon's silver beams guide their whimsical flight,
While secrets of old dance in soft twilight.
They play with the shadows, they hide, then they flee,
In a playground of magic, only they see.

With every soft flicker, a story anew,
Of realms hidden deep in the night's velvet hue.
A tapestry woven with threads of delight,
The dance of the faeries, a mesmerizing sight.

So if you should wander where the wild things roam,
Keep your heart open, let the dreams call you home.
For within every twinkle, each whisper, each sweep,
Lies the dance of the faery spirits, deep in their sleep.

# Glowing Fragments of Forgotten Tales

In corners of twilight, where shadows reside,
Lie glowing fragments of tales long denied.
Whispers of stories, in dust they are spun,
Forgotten yet waiting, for eyes to be won.

They flicker like candles, igniting the past,
With echoes of laughter that long have been cast.
The stories of lovers, of battles and strife,
Imprinted on pages, they dance back to life.

Through thickets of memory, they softly parade,
A gallery rich, where history's laid.
In moonlit reflections, the truth shimmers bright,
Enveloping dreams in the cloak of the night.

Hold tight to the moments, let them be known,
In the fabric of time, our hearts have been sewn.
With every soft flicker, each starlit refrain,
Lives the magic of memories, released from their chain.

So wander this pathway with heart open wide,
Collect glowing fragments, let them be your guide.
For in the soft glow of those stories retold,
Lie the echoes of wonder, forever behold.

## Luminescent Echoes in Mystic Woods

Whispers call from trees so grand,
Where moonlit secrets gently stand.
Shadows dance with silver light,
Guiding souls through cloaked night.

Leaves murmur tales of ages past,
With roots that hold enchantments cast.
Faint echoes swirl in twilight's breath,
Binding magic, life, and death.

A brook sings softly to the stars,
As dreams wander beyond the bars.
Each flicker tells a story true,
In woods where ancient wonders brew.

Faint laughter drifts on cool night air,
With wonder lurking everywhere.
Underneath the watchful gaze,
Of sentinels in a misty haze.

Through paths unknown, the heart will roam,
Finding all it longs to own.
With every step, a spell unfolds,
In Luminescent woods of old.

# Fluttering Shadows of Mythical Beings

In twilight's grip, they weave and sway,
With delicate grace, they drift away.
A flutter here, a whisper there,
Magic lingers in the air.

Winged figures in the gloaming light,
Dancing softly, out of sight.
They speak in colors vivid and bright,
Filling the heart with pure delight.

Their laughter rings like crystal bells,
Weaving stories, casting spells.
In forests deep, where dreams ignite,
Lost within their mystic flight.

Each shadow holds a hidden tale,
Of wonders that will never pale.
Through whispered songs, they guide our way,
Chasing dawn through night's ballet.

Under stars, they find their tune,
With starlit trails drawn by the moon.
Fluttering shadows, ever near,
In mythical realms, they appear.

# Fireflies in the Realm of Whimsy

In tangled grass and blooms that sway,
Fireflies dance at close of day.
Glimmers twinkle, so divine,
Lighting up the evening's shrine.

A flicker here, a glow to chase,
In the night's warm embrace.
These tiny sparks bring tales of old,
Of hidden dreams and secrets told.

With every flick, a wish takes flight,
Carried on the wind of night.
Through the garden, laughter flows,
As whimsical wonders softly grow.

The moonbeams join the playful game,
Illuminating paths aflame.
With magic bursting in each hue,
Fireflies sharing tales anew.

In the realm where fancy plays,
Life enchants in myriad ways.
In shimmering light, the heart will see,
A world alive with jubilee.

# Celestial Riddles in the Nightshade

Beneath the cloak of velvet skies,
Stars glimmer with knowing eyes.
Each one a riddle, a tale concealed,
In the vastness, mysteries revealed.

Nightshade blooms in shadows deep,
Cradling secrets that softly seep.
In silver beams, the cosmos sings,
Of worlds beyond and timeless things.

Whispers echo across the field,
In the silence, answers yield.
Galaxies spin with stories rare,
Entwined in the cool night air.

Lost in thoughts of ages past,
Held in the charm of starlight cast.
Each flicker brings a haunting grace,
Unraveling time in this sacred space.

Celestial riddles beckon near,
Carried on a breath, pure and clear.
In nightshade's grasp, we unlock the dream,
Beneath the cosmos' shimmering beam.

## Breaching the Veil of Twinkling Night

In shadows deep, where whispers weave,
Stars alight, a fate to believe.
Moonlight spills like silken threads,
Neath the watchful gaze of the dead.

Echoes of dreams in the twilight glow,
Secrets bound in the winds that blow.
A dance of sighs, a promise spoken,
In realms where hearts remain unbroken.

Wonders kaleidoscopic unfold,
As stories of courage in silence told.
Tales of magic entwined in the air,
Unfurling beneath our timeless stare.

With every breath, we breathe in the skies,
Veils lifted as the night slowly sighs.
In this realm, where dreams take flight,
We find our truth in the twinkling night.

# Fables Written in Light's Quill

Beneath the arch of golden sun,
Whispers dance, adventures begun.
Ink of starlight, on parchment fair,
Crafting legends beyond compare.

Every shimmer, a tale to tell,
Of heroes rising, of shadows that fell.
A quill of hope on paper bright,
Etching fables in the fading light.

In the quiet ink of the evening's grace,
Time weaves stories in a gentle embrace.
With pages turning like leaves in flight,
Each word a treasure, burning bright.

From distant lands, a voice calls near,
A symphony wild, yet crystal clear.
With every verse, the heart may thrill,
For life itself is written by light's quill.

## Glimmers of Hope in the Woodland Dusk

In the hushed heart of the forest deep,
Where shadows linger and secrets sleep.
Glimmers of hope between the trees,
Whispering tales borne on the breeze.

As twilight drapes its velvet cloak,
Nature's breath, a soothing choke.
Stars peek through the cloak of night,
Dancing softly in gentle light.

A robin sings a lonesome tune,
Hopeful echoes of afternoon.
With every note, the dusk abides,
In wild harmony, the darkness hides.

And in the quiet, lies a spark,
A promise glowing in the dark.
With each heartbeat, wild and free,
We find our way, just you and me.

## A Symphony of Light and Laughter

In the glade where shadows twirl,
Joy and mirth around us swirl.
Laughter bursts like bubbles bright,
Warming hearts within the night.

Each note a melody, sweetly sung,
In the symphony of the young.
Dancing leaves, a giddy plight,
Beneath the soft embrace of light.

With every giggle, the stars align,
Magic weaves a tale divine.
Echoes of joy in the evening's thrall,
A chorus of hope, inviting all.

In this moment, time stands still,
A spark ignites, the heart to fill.
And under the watch of the moon's soft glow,
We dance through dreams, where laughter flows.

## Luminous Dreams in the Heart of the Woods

In the depths where whispers dwell,
A misty song begins to swell,
Moonlight weaves through ancient trees,
Carrying secrets on the breeze.

Strange shadows dance upon the ground,
With every step, new worlds are found,
Wildflowers bloom in shades so rare,
Guiding wanderers unaware.

The silver brook sings soft and low,
Its rippling tales in gentle flow,
Close your eyes, let your heart steer,
For luminous dreams are ever near.

Awake the magic, let it spread,
In forest glades where few have tread,
Let the stars light your fateful way,
In the heart of woods, where night holds sway.

So linger long, let your spirit twine,
In this realm where dreams align,
For every step is a vow you keep,
In luminous dreams, where shadows leap.

# The Enchanted Glow of Hidden Paths

Through thickets thick, where few have walked,
The air is pulsed with magic's talk,
Leaves shimmer with an otherworld glow,
In whispers soft, they tell secrets low.

Follow the trails brushed in gold light,
Where time bends, and stars touch night,
Secrets coil in each bend and turn,
Patience required, for wisdom to earn.

Beneath the boughs, old tales unfold,
Legends of love, and spirits bold,
In every shadow, in every beam,
The heart can weave the wildest dream.

A flicker here, a glimmer there,
A breeze that dances, light as air,
On hidden paths where few have trod,
You'll meet the quiet, knowing god.

So step with care, let wonder thieve,
For in this light, you may believe,
That magic glows on every hill,
The enchanted glow awaits your will.

# Flickering Lanterns of the Otherworld

Among the fog where shadows play,
Flickering lanterns light the way,
In spectral hues, they beckon near,
Guiding souls both lost and clear.

With every flicker, stories rise,
Echoing through the midnight skies,
Their whispers swirl in twilight's grace,
Inviting dreams to find their place.

Once weary hearts, now filled with light,
Transcend the veil of star-kissed night,
In the embrace of ghostly glow,
To places where the brave may go.

While jests of fate interlace the scene,
Time unravels in threads unseen,
The lanterns guide with tender might,
Flickering softly, warm and bright.

So join the dance, partake the lore,
With flickering lanterns, seek the door,
To realms where magic takes its flight,
In the heart of shadows wrapped in light.

## Radiance in the Twilight of the Fae

In twilight's grasp, a shimmer glows,
Where fae folk roam in endless rows,
Their laughter twines with evening sighs,
As magic blooms beneath the skies.

Crickets chirp a twilight tune,
Beneath the watchful silver moon,
Soft glimmers dance upon the grass,
In every moment, fae spirits pass.

As shadows stretch and candles burn,
The night reveals what dreams can learn,
A tapestry of glistening light,
A radiant world of pure delight.

Let your heart be still and wide,
In fae realms where wonders bide,
For every shadow hides a spark,
In the radiance of the dark.

Explore with care, with spirits free,
In twilight's glow, find harmony,
The fae invite you to their dance,
In radiant nights, where dreams entrance.

### The Glint of Starlight Kisses

In the hush of night's embrace,
Stars whisper tales of grace.
Moonbeams weave a silver thread,
Cradling dreams, where wishes tread.

Each twinkle speaks a secret tune,
A soft caress from the silver moon.
Hearts ignite with a fleeting glow,
Beneath the heavens, where wonders flow.

Glimmers dance in sapphire skies,
As midnight magic gently sighs.
Every flicker holds a plea,
To cherish all that's yet to be.

In this realm of midnight's kiss,
We find a taste of timeless bliss.
A moment's pause, a breath's delight,
Wrapped in the glint of starlit night.

So let your heart take flight and soar,
Where dreams are spun forevermore.
In starlight's embrace, we're intertwined,
Infinite love, heart and mind.

# Smoldering Hues of Sylvan Secrets

Whispers weave through ancient trees,
Secrets spoken with the breeze.
Golden leaves, a quiet fire,
Ignite the soul, set hearts higher.

In twilight hours, the shadows play,
A dance of dusk at end of day.
Mocha browns and ruby reds,
Cradle life where magic treads.

Hushed beneath the emerald canopies,
Voices linger like sweet melodies.
Traces of dreams in every shade,
In sylvan depths, a bond is laid.

A tapestry of nature's art,
Crafts an ember in the heart.
Within these woods, the spirits roam,
In the warm hues, we find our home.

Let your spirit wander free,
Among the dying leaves and glee.
For in these woods, the heart finds peace,
In smoldering hues, our joys increase.

## Spirits Light the Way in Faerie Rings

In a circle of enchanted glow,
Whispers of bygone tales do flow.
Each step carries a gentle charm,
In faerie rings where dreams disarm.

Glimmering lights weave through the air,
Soft laughter slipping everywhere.
A mystical dance beneath the trees,
Where every heart is set at ease.

The spirits beckon with twinkling eyes,
Drawing you in to the ancient ties.
They lift you high on wings of delight,
In the embrace of the moon's soft light.

Each ring holds wisdom from times gone past,
A promise whispered, always to last.
As laughter echoes in the serene night,
We find our way in the faerie light.

So take a chance, let your heart foresee,
The wonders waiting, wild and free.
In every circle, a memory sings,
As spirits light the way on wondrous wings.

# Glowing Laughter in the Moonlit Grove

Beneath the boughs where shadows sway,
Laughter glows at end of day.
Moonlit beams like tender sighs,
Lift spirits high to starlit skies.

In a grove where secrets thrive,
Glows a warmth that feels alive.
Every chuckle, bright and clear,
Brings the stars a little near.

A tapestry of joy unfolds,
In playful whispers, magic molds.
Dance and twirl, let laughter soar,
In this grove, you'll ask for more.

Each echo spins a golden thread,
Binding hearts wherever led.
The moon watches with a knowing smile,
Encouraging joy to linger awhile.

So gather close, let worries fade,
In the warmth of laughter, serenade.
For in this grove, beneath the light,
We find our joys, our hearts take flight.

# Enigmatic Lights in the Woodland's Embrace

In the hush of twilight's call,
Flickers dance, both shy and small.
Whispers weave through ancient trees,
Mysteries stirred by the gentle breeze.

Shadows cast in hues of gold,
Stories of the wild retold.
Each glint a secret, softly spun,
Beneath the gaze of the setting sun.

Footsteps hush on mossy ground,
In every rustle, magic found.
The woodland breathes with gentle sighs,
As stars awaken in velvet skies.

Casting glows from leaf to stream,
Nature weaves a timeless dream.
Hidden paths where fairies tread,
In enchanted light, all fears are shed.

So wander deep, let heart take flight,
Under the canopy of night.
For in each light, a tale awaits,
In woodland's grasp, where magic creates.

# A Symphony of Sparks Beneath the Canopy

Beneath the boughs, a song does play,
With every flicker, night turns to day.
Sparks like notes on silken strings,
In this grove where wonder springs.

The moonlight waltzes with the leaves,
As evening whispers softly weaves.
A lullaby of twinkling lights,
Guiding lost hearts back to heights.

With trails of amber, paths unfold,
Secrets of the forest gold.
Echoes dance in the cool night air,
A symphony that bids us care.

Each firefly a note, a beat,
In the symphony, both calming and sweet.
As woodland creatures join along,
Their hearts attuned to nature's song.

So listen close, let spirits rise,
In rustling leaves, find the skies.
A melody of stars above,
Playing softly, the tune of love.

# Wandering Glimmers in the Land of the Fae

In twilight's brush, where shadows cling,
Glimmers dance as fairies sing.
A secret realm, both bright and rare,
Where whispers float upon the air.

Mossy carpets, emerald hues,
Guide the wanderers, old and new.
With every flicker, hopes ignite,
In the embrace of fading light.

Beneath the arch of twilight's dome,
These glimmers beckon weary home.
A tapestry of dreams unfolds,
In the land where magic holds.

With laughter light as petals fall,
Innocence dances, answering the call.
Each spark a story, a tale so grand,
Woven together by fate's gentle hand.

So seek the paths where fae tread light,
In every spark, there rests delight.
For in their glow, old worlds collide,
In wandering glimmers, dreams abide.

# Echoes of Light in Forgotten Glens

In forgotten glens, where echoes play,
Light weaves stories of the day.
Gentle gleams on dewy leaves,
Whispers of the past, the heart believes.

The sun's soft rays through branches filter,
Painting shadows, soft and siltier.
Each ray reveals a long-lost truth,
A fleeting glimpse of eternal youth.

With every step on winding trails,
Echoing laughter in the gales.
Memories linger, lost yet found,
In every creak of the enchanted ground.

Beneath the boughs, stories rest,
In the glow, the forest's best.
Ancient spirits roam, unseen,
Guiding wanderers to where they've been.

So pause awhile, let time unfold,
In forgotten glens, embrace the bold.
For echoes of light invite the quest,
In nature's arms, the heart finds rest.

# A Tapestry of Light in the Faery Haven

In a glen where silence sings,
Softly dance the faery sprites.
Their laughter spins on whispering winds,
A tapestry of shimmering lights.

Petals glow with dew's caress,
While shadows twinkle like the stars.
The heartbeats of the forest press,
As magic whispers through the bars.

Beneath the boughs of ancient trees,
The air is thick with secrets spun.
Every rustle brings a breeze,
A song of dusk when day is done.

In twilight's arms, they weave their dreams,
Through moonlit paths of silken threads.
Where light and shadow softly gleam,
In her embrace, no heart dreads.

A dance of light in faery halls,
Where evenings stretch to endless nights.
With every echo, wonder calls,
In the haven of twinkling sights.

## Flickering Dreams in Sylvan Glades

In sylvan glades where shadows play,
Flickering dreams take delicate flight.
The whispers of the leaves convey,
A symphony painted in twilight's light.

Crickets chirp their evening tune,
As stars awaken one by one.
Beneath a silken, crescent moon,
The forest wraps in twilight's fun.

Each glimmer holds a tale untold,
Of brave adventures lost in time.
With every shimmer, hearts dare bold,
To reach for magic in their prime.

In quiet glades where spirits dwell,
Opal dreams slip through the air.
In each flicker, a secret spell,
Awakens hope for hearts that dare.

Through tangled roots and brambled ways,
The dreams of night entwine with glee.
In sylvan glades, 'neath starry rays,
The flickering moments set us free.

## Whispered Light Beneath the Moon's Embrace

Whispered light drapes soft and low,
Beneath the moon's enchanted gaze.
In silvered beams, the shadows flow,
Like echoes in an evening haze.

Nightingales serenade the night,
Their songs weave through the velvet air.
And in the glow, all feels just right,
As dreams dissolve all earthly care.

The ancient trees in silence stand,
Guardians of secrets draped in shade.
With every rustle, take my hand,
And let us wander unafraid.

Beneath this dome of twinkling stars,
We'll chase the wishes in the night.
In delicate laughter, we'll find our scars,
And heal our hearts with whispered light.

As dawn approaches, shadows fade,
Yet in our hearts, the magic stays.
In moon's embrace, we boldly wade,
Where whispered dreams light all our ways.

# Gossamer Flickers in Enchanted Fields

In enchanted fields where shadows weave,
Gossamer flickers dance and sway.
They twirl on whispers of dreams perceived,
And linger in the twilight's play.

With every breath, the night unfolds,
As twilight paints the canvas bright.
Each flicker glimmers, softly bold,
In secret corners kissed by light.

The grass hums low with secrets shared,
While starlight bathes the earth in grace.
In this embrace, no heart is scared,
As we find home in nature's space.

A symphony of colors blend,
Where light and dark forever chase.
In every twist, a tale to send,
With gossamer threads of fleeting grace.

As daylight breaks, the flickers wane,
Yet memories dance beneath the sky.
In enchanted fields, we'll meet again,
Where dreams are born and never die.

## Celestial Flashes Among Dreamers

In realms where whispers linger light,
The starlit dreams take flight at night.
Each glittering thought, a fragile thread,
Weaving the hopes that dance ahead.

Bright constellations smile and gleam,
Guiding the lost on paths of dream.
Where shadows play in silver beams,
Awakening hearts with silent screams.

Misty clouds conceal their grace,
In shimmering depths, we find our place.
The universe sings in vibrant hues,
A canvas rich with mystic views.

With every heartbeat, magic flows,
In secret spaces where the starlight glows.
Each twinkle beckons, soft and sweet,
Inviting souls to rise and meet.

This dance of dreams, a cosmic waltz,
In celestial flashes, we find our faults.
Yet in the stardust, bright and bold,
Lie tales of wonder yet untold.

# Night's Canvas Decorated with Sparks


A tapestry of midnight blue,
Adorned with diamonds, fresh and new.
The moon spills secrets with soft sighs,
As ancient worlds awaken, rise.

Across the heavens, vibrant threads,
Stitching the dreams still buzz in heads,
Every flicker a whispered prayer,
Binding the lost with gentle care.

Wanderers pause beneath the glow,
In awe of wonders, tales they know.
Each spark a story, pure and bright,
Illuminating the edge of night.

From shadowed realms where phantoms roam,
To glowing orbs that call us home.
Every heartbeat, a pulse so strong,
In the night's chorus, we belong.

These cosmic strokes of fate and chance,
Guide us gently in a timeless dance.
Awake to beauty, let hearts ignite,
In night's canvas, we can recite.

# Radiance in the Domain of Mischief

Where laughter echoes, shadows dart,
In realms of mischief, a lively heart.
Pixies flit in a playful haze,
Shimmering trails of bright displays.

Every corner holds a sly delight,
With whispers stirring in soft twilight.
A world adorned in color's play,
With secrets woven near and far away.

The moon grins down on pranks well-laid,
As dreaming minds in twilight wade.
With every giggle, a spark ignites,
Awakening magic from tranquil nights.

Jests and japes in the glimmering air,
Invite the brave to join the dare.
In a dance of twinkling effervescent glee,
Where merry hearts soar wild and free.

Embrace the realm where mischief reigns,
With laughter woven through joy and pains.
Here, we find our radiant space,
In the domain of mischief, we find our grace.

## Enchanted Glades and Fabled Twinklings

In glades where gentle breezes sigh,
Your heart can flutter, and spirits fly.
Each blade of grass a tale untold,
Painting the world in hues of gold.

Fabled twinklings in the air,
Hint at treasures hidden with care.
The trees, they whisper secrets old,
Of knights and dragons, brave and bold.

Mossy paths invite your feet,
To wander where enchantments greet.
A gentle stream sings soft refrain,
In tranquil notes that wash away pain.

The twilight dances, shadows sway,
In enchanted glades, dreams come play.
Each glance a shimmer, each laugh a spark,
Guiding the way through the tender dark.

With every heartbeat, the magic binds,
In whispers of the heart's desires.
Embrace this night, let your spirit find,
The fabled twinklings of kindred minds.

# Ethereal Gales with Glowing Tails

Whispering winds through the trees,
Dancing shadows in the night.
Glimmers of magic, carried with ease,
In the heart of the moon's soft light.

Gentle breezes weave a tale,
Of secrets held in starlit skies.
With every breath, the spirits sail,
A symphony of whispered sighs.

Flickering fireflies paint the air,
Their glowing tails a fleeting dream.
Amongst the silence, a whispered prayer,
To the gales that weave and beam.

Nature hums her timeless song,
Echoing through the twilight gleam.
In this realm where we belong,
A world that feels like waking dream.

Ethereal gales, forever true,
Guide our hearts to realms anew.
In the night, the magic flows,
With glowing tails, our spirits rose.

# Breaths of Light in the Woodland Silence

In the hush of dusk, soft and light,
Breaths of wonder drift along.
A tapestry woven, dark from bright,
Nature sings a silent song.

Mossy paths where fairies tread,
Glimmering seeds in hidden glades.
With every leap, new dreams are bred,
In the shrine of ancient shades.

Crickets chirp, a melody sweet,
Notes entwining with the trees.
Nature's pulse, a gentle beat,
Breaths of light in the whispering breeze.

Moonbeams dance on silver streams,
Lucent trails of fate and chance.
In woodland silence, we find dreams,
A haven lost in night's romance.

Magic swirls in the cool, crisp air,
Inviting all to take their flight.
In woodland realms, we shed our care,
With breaths of light, we greet the night.

# Dappled Illumination in the Witching Hour

Underneath a cloak of dark,
Dappled light begins to play.
Whispers echo, leaving a mark,
In the shadows, dreams portray.

Flickering lanterns softly glow,
Curving paths through ancient trees.
Where the secrets of night do flow,
In the heart of a silent breeze.

Tales of witches, spun from light,
Mingling under the crescent moon.
In the stillness of the night,
Magic stirs, a haunting tune.

Illumination weaves the air,
A tapestry of verdant dreams.
Calling spirits, wild and rare,
Beneath the sky, the starlight beams.

In the witching hour's embrace,
Mysteries linger, watch and wait.
With dappled light, we find our place,
In a world that whispers fate.

# Luminescent Whims of the Enchanted Grove

In the grove where wonders twine,
Luminescence paints the leaves.
Glowing whims, both bright and fine,
Entice the heart and spirit believes.

Rustling leaves, a joyful sound,
Bubbles of laughter drift afar.
In this place where dreams abound,
Magic glimmers like a star.

Twinkling lights on branches sway,
Summer's breath, a fragrant kiss.
Guiding footsteps as they play,
In a realm of purest bliss.

With every turn, a secret found,
In shadows cast by moonlit beams.
Echoes of enchantment abound,
Awakening the lost of dreams.

Underneath a vaulted sky,
Where luminescent visions dance.
In the enchanted grove, we sigh,
Surrendering to evening's trance.

# Glimmering Shadows in Enchanted Glades

In glades where shadows softly dance,
The faerie lights begin to prance.
With whispers lost in evening's haze,
The world is wrapped in silken days.

Beneath the boughs of ancient trees,
A symphony of rustling leaves.
In twilight's grasp, enchantments bloom,
As magic weaves its gentle loom.

From crystal streams, reflections gleam,
Each ripple tells a secret dream.
The shadows weave, a tale unspoken,
In glimmering glades, the silence broken.

With every breath, the heart takes flight,
In harmony with stars so bright.
The air is thick with dreams untold,
In glimmering shadows, courage bold.

So wander softly, tread with care,
For in these woods, the wonders flare.
Embrace the night and all its charms,
In enchanted glades, find magic's arms.

# Twinkling Flames in the Woodland Night

The forest stirs, a vibrant song,
Where twinkling flames of dusk belong.
Each leaf aglow, a gilded sight,
As dreams ignite in woodland night.

Beneath the stars, a fire's cheer,
The air is warm, the heart is near.
In whispered tales, the embers soar,
To light the paths forevermore.

The crackling sparks, a joyful dance,
Each flicker holds a fleeting chance.
To remember all the bold desires,
That flicker softly like the fires.

A midnight feast with friends so true,
With wildwood scents, the forest's brew.
In laughter's echo, spirits rise,
And twinkling flames reveal the skies.

As shadows wane and dawn draws near,
The woodland whispers, calm and clear.
Hold close the warmth, the magic bright,
In every heart, twinkling light.

# Whispers of Light Beneath the Moonlit Canopy

Beneath the boughs of emerald grace,
The moonlight casts a timeless trace.
With whispers soft, the night awakes,
In silvery hues, the daylight breaks.

The stars, they shimmer, secrets share,
In shadows deep, a gentle prayer.
For in the hush, our spirits soar,
Through moonlit paths, forevermore.

Each rustling leaf, a tale retold,
Of ancient bonds and magic bold.
With every step, enchantment swells,
In whispers of light, the heart compels.

So gather close, dear friends of night,
In harmony, we find our light.
For in the dance of dreams we weave,
In moonlit songs, our hopes believe.

The canopy holds mysteries bright,
In echoes soft of pure delight.
So linger long, let magic stay,
In whispers sweet, we'll find our way.

# Luminescent Threads in the Faery Realm

In the realm where faeries play,
Luminescent threads weave day to day.
With shimmered dreams and laughter grand,
Life bursts forth from the heart of the land.

Each thread, a story, bright and new,
A tapestry of every hue.
In twilight's glow, joys intertwine,
In secret glades, our souls align.

As starlit rivers gently flow,
In whispers sweet, their magic shows.
The dance of light in twilight's grace,
Each luminous thread finds its place.

Through fields of wild, where shadows sway,
The night's embrace guides us on the way.
In faery realms, we share our dreams,
With threads of hope that softly gleam.

So gather 'round, and hold on tight,
To luminescent threads of light.
For in this realm where hearts unite,
We'll weave our stories, bold and bright.

# The Whispering Woods' Glowed Delight

In the woods where shadows play,
Silent whispers dance by day.
Leaves aglow with emerald light,
Magic weaves through day and night.

Mysteries beneath the trees,
Gentle laughter in the breeze.
Branches sway with tales untold,
Secrets hidden, yet so bold.

Ferns unfurl in soft embrace,
Warmth and wonder find their place.
Fairy trails and glimmering streams,
Echo softly, framing dreams.

Every footstep, a step to lore,
Every rustle opens more.
Nature sings a soft refrain,
In the woods, we'll dream again.

As dusk settles, stars take flight,
Branches cradle the dying light.
In this grove, where spirits soar,
Whispered wishes ask for more.

## Wandering Sparks Beneath the Stars

Glimmers dance in the midnight cool,
Where wishes echo, like a school.
Each star a map, a dream to chase,
Under the vast, enchanting space.

Footsteps soft on dew-kissed grass,
Time stands still, moments pass.
With every breath, the cosmos hums,
Calling hearts to where joy thrums.

Wandering sparks, they light the way,
Leading souls who dare to stray.
On paths glistening with silver hues,
In the night, they share their muse.

Gentle breezes whisper low,
Promises held in the night's glow.
Clouds like pillows float above,
Carrying our dreams of love.

Wrapped in dreams, we twirl and spin,
With the stars, we lose and win.
Underneath this canopy bright,
We wander through the endless night.

# Flickers of Joy in the Glade of Secrets

In the glade where shadows meet,
Joy flickers softly, bittersweet.
Petals whisper tales of old,
In colors vibrant, brave and bold.

Sunlight dapples through the trees,
Nestled whispers in the breeze.
Hidden laughter, ever near,
In the glade, there's naught to fear.

Squirrels scamper, playing games,
Nature's stage, with no claims.
Secrets cradled in each nook,
Find the joy within the book.

Every shadow holds a tale,
Every breeze tells stories pale.
Flickering lights, a gentle sway,
Guiding spirits to where they play.

In this haven, hearts align,
Where dreams and laughter intertwine.
In the glade, we find our way,
Flickers of joy in soft ballet.

# The Hidden Glow of the Woodland's Heart

In the heart where whispers glow,
Mysteries of the woodland flow.
Roots entwined in tales of yore,
Nature's secrets at the core.

Mossy carpets, soft as sighs,
Echo tales beneath the skies.
Each rustling leaf, a gentle voice,
In the stillness, hearts rejoice.

Winding paths of ancient lore,
Lead us to the hidden door.
Where time itself cannot intrude,
In the depths, we find our mood.

Fireflies blink, like stars anew,
In this realm, where dreams break through.
Golden glimmers, soft and bright,
Illuminate the tranquil night.

Take a breath, and you will see,
The woodland's heart can set you free.
In the glow, we dance and twine,
Hidden magic, yours and mine.

## Dreamweaver's Glow in Faerie Realm

In the realm where dreams take flight,
Whispers dance on wings of light.
Stars entwined with moonlit dew,
Every heartbeat sings anew.

Gossamer trails of laughter roam,
Guiding lost souls to their home.
Softly spun from twilight's loom,
A tapestry of night's perfume.

Beneath the boughs where shadows wane,
Secrets whisper, soft refrain.
With every flicker of the glow,
The faerie magic starts to flow.

Crickets serenade the skies,
As twilight's veil begins to rise.
In kingdoms crafted from a sigh,
Dreamweavers weave their wishes high.

A symphony of night unfolds,
In every twinkle, truth beholds.
With every breath, imagine this,
A world adorned in faerie bliss.

## Radiant Footprints of the Wild

In tangled woods where secrets hide,
Radiant footsteps softly glide.
Nature's heart beats strong and bold,
With stories waiting to be told.

Sun-kissed leaves in gentle sway,
Mark the paths where creatures play.
Each print a tale of wanderlust,
In every shadow, dreams we trust.

Mushrooms sprout in vibrant hues,
Crafting magic in the dew.
With every heartbeat in the breeze,
The forest hums in melodies.

From babbling brooks to starlit skies,
Nature whispers, never lies.
In every rustle, every sigh,
The wildest wonders softly lie.

A dance of light on petals bright,
Nature calls with pure delight.
Embrace the call of the wild, my friend,
In the radiant footsteps, let us blend.

## Whims of Dusk and Glow

As dusk unfurls her velvet hue,
Golden glimmers start anew.
The world transforms in twilight's grace,
Where dreams and reality embrace.

Winds of whimsy weave their tale,
On twilight's breath, we set to sail.
Each flicker holds a story's spark,
In shadows deep, we roam the dark.

Fireflies dance in rhythmic bliss,
A waltz of light, a fleeting kiss.
Beneath the moon's enchanting gaze,
We lose ourselves in hazy maze.

With every sigh, the stars awake,
In azure skies, our hearts partake.
Whispers echo, secrets flow,
In the whims of dusk and glow.

Embracing night, we chase our dreams,
In silken threads, reality gleams.
With every heartbeat, shadows wane,
In the dance of dusk, joy we gain.

# Threads of Light on Evening's Breath

In the silent hush of fall's embrace,
Threads of light weave through time and space.
Echoes of laughter in moonlit pools,
The canvas shifts, where magic rules.

Stars like jewels in velvet skies,
Glisten softly, like whispered sighs.
Nature cradles evening's glow,
In every breath, the world will flow.

With shadows playing hide and seek,
The night unfolds, soft and meek.
Mysteries linger in every corner,
Drawing dreamers into wonder.

The nightingale sings a tender lull,
In quiet corners, hearts are full.
Each note a wish, a dream unfurled,
Threads of light, our secret world.

As dawn approaches, softly treads,
We weave our tales, where hope is bred.
In evening's breath, magic alive,
In every heart, new dreams arrive.

## The Flicker and Dance of Sylvan Spirits

In twilight's grasp, they weave and sway,
Soft whispers in the fading day.
With laughter sweet, they twirl around,
A melody of life profound.

Through ancient trees, their shadows spill,
A fleeting breath, a haunting thrill.
Glimmers bright, like stars alight,
They dance and fade into the night.

In sparkling pools, their secrets hide,
Where moonbeams touch, and dreams abide.
A world apart, yet close they roam,
In nature's heart, they find their home.

With each soft flutter, hearts shall soar,
To realms unknown, forevermore.
Ethereal beings, in magic cloaked,
Through mossy glades, their laughter choked.

So wander deep where shadows lead,
And listen close, for hearts that breed,
The flicker and dance of sylvan dreams,
In every rustle, a soul redeems.

# Mystic Luminescence in the Realm of Dreams

In dreams we tread on silver strands,
Where time slips through ungrasped hands.
A tapestry of whispered sighs,
Beneath the veil of starry skies.

A glow unfolds, both soft and bright,
In the hush of dark, a gentle light.
With each heartbeat, the magic swells,
In silent woods where enchantment dwells.

The echoes of a distant chime,
Awake the spirit, lost in rhyme.
Illusions dance on moonlit waves,
In secret realms, the heart enslaves.

The shadows blend with colors rare,
As hopes take flight on whispered air.
Mystic paths of dreams entwined,
In every corner, magic primed.

So close your eyes, let go the day,
And drift where silver dreams hold sway.
In the realm where visions gleam,
Embrace the mystic, blissful dream.

## Twinkling Spirits in the Gossamer Boughs

In gossamer threads, they softly sway,
Twinkling spirits at end of day.
Their laughter drapes the twilight sky,
In hidden nooks where fairies fly.

With glimmers bright, they weave and spin,
A dance of joy where dreams begin.
Among the leaves, so fresh and green,
Their vibrant forms are rarely seen.

On gentle winds, they whisper low,
Secrets of the earth they know.
With every flicker in the night,
Hope awakens, burning bright.

In silvered light, they take their flight,
A symphony of pure delight.
Through branches high, they flit and play,
A tapestry of night and day.

So lift your gaze to dappled skies,
And find the spark where magic lies.
In twinkling spirits, hearts shall grow,
In every bough, a tale to show.

## Celestial Radiance on the Forest Floor

Where ancient trees stretch towards the stars,
The forest floor holds hidden bars.
A radiant glow, like morning dew,
Brings life anew, as shadows strew.

In every petal, a story glows,
Of whispered winds and gentle flows.
Celestial lights, they dance and weave,
In every heart, a thread to leave.

Underneath the verdant shield,
A realm unfolds, a dream revealed.
With every step on tangled way,
The pulse of earth begins to play.

The hushed embrace of dusk's caress,
In twilight's song, the world's finesse.
With open hearts, we seek and find,
The radiant whispers, intertwined.

So wander deep where magic pours,
With every breath, the spirit soars.
In celestial warmth that gently calls,
On the forest floor, the beauty falls.

## Flickering Hues Amongst the Elf's Whisper

In twilight's glow, the shadows play,
Soft whispers drift where fairies sway.
A tapestry woven with light so bright,
Colors emerge from the deepening night.

Dancing beams through the leaves do weave,
Wonders abound, if one would believe.
Glimmers of gold, and silver so rare,
A secret world beyond all compare.

Around each tree, a story to tell,
In flickering hues, where magics dwell.
With every breath, the night sings low,
Songs of the forest, soft and aglow.

## Celestial Flickers Beneath Ancient Boughs

Beneath the sky where the stars are torn,
Ancient boughs whisper of tales reborn.
Flickers of light from the heavens cascade,
Illuminating mysteries, long since laid.

The moon drapes silver on the forest floor,
Painting the shadows, forevermore.
Each glow a promise, each sparkle a dream,
In the embrace of the night's gentle beam.

Moss carpets the ground in a velvet spread,
Where dreams take flight and the lost are led.
Celestial secrets in rustling leaves,
Breathe in the magic, the heart believes.

## The Dance of Lights in Sylvan Secrets

In hollowed glens where the shadows prance,
The fireflies twinkle in a joyful dance.
A rhythm of night, a melody sweet,
With every flicker, the world feels replete.

Branches sway gently in the night air,
Swirling with echoes of secrets laid bare.
The symphony plays as the stars align,
In their cosmic waltz, a tale divine.

With whispers of gossamer threads spun tight,
Tracing soft paths in the hush of the night.
The dance of lights beneath the dark sky,
Awakens the wonders in hearts passing by.

## Ethereal Sparks Above the Dew-Kissed Moss

Above the moss where the morning glows,
Ethereal sparks in the twilight pose.
Dew-kissed petals brace for the dawn,
As dreams take flight, and the night moves on.

A ballet of colors, soft and bright,
Cascading down from the heavens' height.
In whispers of dawn, the world comes alive,
Each twinkle a promise, the heart will strive.

Amidst the ferns where the wild things roam,
Sparks of enchantment make nature their home.
The tapestry weaves through each waking hour,
In sunlight and shadows, behold the power.

# Luminous Secrets of the Fey

In shadows where the whispers dwell,
The fey weave tales of magic's spell.
With laughter light as evening's breeze,
They guard their secrets 'neath the trees.

A glimmer here, a shimmer there,
Illuminates the moonlit air.
With wings like gossamer, bright and free,
They dance in realms we cannot see.

In hidden groves where flowers bloom,
The fey craft wonders in the gloom.
Their laughter echoes through the night,
A joyous song, a pure delight.

They twirl in rings of silver light,
In every heart, they spark the bright.
Unlocking dreams with a single glance,
They weave our hopes into their dance.

With every secret that they share,
Magic lingers in the air.
For in the depths of moonlit glades,
Luminous secrets never fade.

# Ethereal Sparks Amongst the Elders

In ancient woods where wise ones dwell,
With craggy bark, and stories to tell.
The elders nod with solemn grace,
As sparks of magic fill the space.

Their eyes like orbs of knowing light,
Reflect the depths of endless night.
With gnarled hands and roots so deep,
They watch the world and quietly keep.

With every dawn, they share their lore,
In whispered tales of times before.
Ethereal sparks, they cast so bright,
Illuminating shadows with insight.

Each fluttering leaf a song of old,
In echoes lingering, tales unfold.
Through time's vast tapestry they weave,
A bond with all who dare believe.

In twilight's glow, their wisdom shines,
Through every heart that seeks the signs.
Elders of the wood, so wise and keen,
Guardians of realms we've never seen.

## Glimmering Pathways of Amber Glow

In twilight's grasp, where lanterns gleam,
Glimmering pathways spark a dream.
With amber glow that softly guides,
A dance of light where magic bides.

The forest whispers secrets low,
As moonbeams paint the earth below.
Each step upon the jeweled ground,
Reveals the wonders all around.

From spectral mists, the spirits rise,
In flashes bright that mesmerize.
They beckon forth, inviting souls,
To wander where the mystery rolls.

In every twist, a tale unfolds,
In glimmering pathways, brave and bold.
Through echoes of the past we roam,
Discovering a world, our home.

With every flicker, every spark,
A journey waits within the dark.
Glimmering pathways lead the way,
To realms where wishes rarely stray.

# Tinkerbells and Twilight's Dance

As twilight falls, the fairies play,
With Tinkerbells that light the way.
Their laughter rings like silver chimes,
In night's embrace, where magic climbs.

On gentle wings of zephyr soft,
They flit and flutter, up aloft.
In shades of pink and midnight blue,
They weave their dreams in skies anew.

Through meadows bright, where shadows blend,
Their joyful dance will never end.
With every spin, a sparkle flies,
A burst of joy that never dies.

In starlit hours, they craft the night,
With beads of glow and hopes so bright.
Tinkerbells kindle the stars' embrace,
An enchanting waltz, a pure grace.

With twilight's cloak, their magic gleams,
In every child who dares to dream.
For in the dance, we find a chance,
To join the fairies in their dance.

## Illuminated Notes of Faerie Stories

In a glimmer where shadows twine,
Each faerie sings a tale divine.
Beneath the moon's soft, silver glow,
Whispers of magic dance and flow.

Through ivy lanes and twilight's sheen,
The secrets of the woods are seen.
With every flicker, sparks ignite,
Stories carried on the night.

Stars like diamonds in the sky,
Glimpse of dreams that never die.
A tapestry of light unfurls,
With each note, a wish it twirls.

Oft in the dark, the heart can roam,
In faerie realms, we find our home.
An orchestra of joy and tears,
Plays sweetly in our wondrous years.

So hear the call, believe the lore,
For faerie tales unlock the door.
In those enchanted moments brief,
We find both solace and belief.

# Dancing Lights in a Sylvan Reverie

Softly twinkle, the lights afloat,
Guiding lost souls on a boat.
In tangled woods where dreams take flight,
Dancing shadows embrace the night.

Beneath a veil of whispering leaves,
Nature hums, and the heart believes.
A waltz of beams through branches split,
In every moment, magic's fit.

Crickets chirp a nighttime score,
While starlit pathways beckon lore.
With every flutter, hearts entwine,
In sylvan realms, the stars align.

Follow the glow where secrets lie,
In hidden glades where wishes sigh.
Let every lamp of hope ignite,
Chasing darkness with pure delight.

So sway with grace in twilight's thrall,
For nature's rhythm enchants us all.
In this reverie, serene and bright,
We lose ourselves in dancing light.

# Enchanted Flames in a Timeless Forest

Flickering embers in a glade,
Where every shadow softly wade.
The forest breathes a fiery song,
In echoes where the heart belongs.

Each spark tells tales of times long past,
In the amber warmth, our hearts are cast.
The trees are wise with age and grace,
In this enchanted, sacred space.

Through golden hues and crimson gleam,
We find our place within the dream.
The flames like stars, alive and free,
A symphony of fire and tree.

In every whisper of the flame,
A promise woven with a name.
With fiery passion, spirits soar,
In nature's glow, we crave for more.

So gather round, and feel the heat,
Where kindred spirits often meet.
In this timeless forest's heart,
Embrace the magic, be a part.

# Radiant Whispers in Nature's Lullaby

In the hush of evening's glow,
Nature hums a sweet, soft flow.
Petals falling, like sighs they drift,
A lullaby, a gentle gift.

With every breeze, a tale is spun,
Underneath the setting sun.
The trees bend low, as if to hear,
The whispers of the earth so near.

Crickets sing to stars above,
An ode to life, to peace, to love.
The river croons a soothing rhyme,
Flowing gently through the line of time.

In twilight's arms, we find our rest,
The world, a canvas, truly blessed.
Let nature's lullaby enfold,
A story quiet, yet so bold.

So close your eyes, in dreams fly high,
With radiant whispers, hearts comply.
In this embrace of night's sweet sigh,
We dance with stars in the sky.

www.ingramcontent.com/pod-product-compliance
Ingram Content Group UK Ltd.
Pitfield, Milton Keynes, MK11 3LW, UK
UKHW021421220125
4239UKWH00007B/187

9 781805 631637